Original title:
Murmurs Beneath the Rainveil's Glow

Copyright © 2025 Swan Charm
All rights reserved.

Author: Paula Raudsepp
ISBN HARDBACK: 978-9908-1-7225-5
ISBN PAPERBACK: 978-9908-1-7226-2
ISBN EBOOK: 978-9908-1-7227-9

Fables from Below the Hazy Arch

In the shadows where whispers play,
Fables weave through the end of day.
A light that flickers, soft and pale,
Tales of wonder in every trail.

Beneath the arch where dreams may float,
A lost song sings in a weathered note.
Every sigh carries a secret wish,
Waiting patiently, like a hidden fish.

Figures dance in the twilight's glow,
Stories of old, the brave and the slow.
With hearts entwined, they gently tread,
Each step a life, each word well-spread.

In the forest of time, shadows cast,
Memories flicker, tied to the past.
Visions murmur, drawing near,
Echoes of laughter, whispers clear.

As stars awaken, dreams unfold,
In reveries wrapped, both timid and bold.
From deep below, the fables rise,
Under the arch, where the truth lies.

Whispers in the Waters' Rhythm

Gentle waves kiss the shore,
Softly singing songs of yore.
In their dance, a tale unfolds,
Secrets of the deep, untold.

Ripples glide beneath the moon,
Each whisper a silvery tune.
Nature's heart beats in the flow,
Echoes of the world we know.

The tides breathe in and out,
In their song, there's no doubt.
Nature's pulse, a calming balm,
A soothing touch, forever calm.

Where the river meets the sea,
There lies a hidden mystery.
Waves harmonize with the wind,
In their rhythms, hope begins.

Lost in time, we drift away,
To the waters' soft ballet.
Whispers in the shadows play,
Guiding dreams till break of day.

Sighs of the Thunderous Sky

Clouds gather with a heavy sigh,
Darkened realms where eagles fly.
Lightning flashes, a brief embrace,
Stormy love, a wild chase.

Thunder rolls like a heartbeat,
In the distance, a fierce greet.
Nature's voice, both gentle and bold,
Whispers of power, stories unfold.

Rain pours down like silken threads,
Kissing ground where life now spreads.
Each droplet a soft, sweet sound,
Washing worries from the ground.

In the chaos, peace we find,
Nature dancing, intertwined.
Against the storm, we stand tall,
In the beauty, we lose our all.

Sighs of sky, a fierce embrace,
Reminding us of nature's grace.
In the thunder's roaring song,
We discover where we belong.

Delicate Notes Amidst the Raindrops

Raindrops fall like whispered tales,
Each one a note that gently trails.
Melodies in the air do play,
Nature's concert on display.

A symphony of soft cascades,
Dance of water, never fades.
Pattering softly on the leaves,
Nature's song, the heart believes.

In puddles, reflections glow,
Tiny worlds where dreams can grow.
Every drop a chance to start,
A delicate work of art.

Listen close to the rain's embrace,
A soothing touch, a gentle grace.
In its rhythm, we find our peace,
In the whispers, our worries cease.

Delicate notes trace the air,
A lullaby for those who dare.
Join the dance, let your spirit soar,
In the rain, we are forever more.

Murmuring Secrets of the Drifting Fog

Fog rolls in, a mystic shroud,
Whispers spoken not aloud.
Secrets hidden in the gray,
Veils of mystery lead the way.

Softly creeping through the night,
Bringing shadows, stealing light.
Each swirl holds a story tight,
In silence, dreams take flight.

Among the trees, it intertwines,
A dance where reality bends and shines.
Murmurs of what's yet to come,
In fog's embrace, we all become.

A gentle hand upon the face,
In its grip, we find our place.
Embrace the hush, let thoughts collide,
In the fog, our fears subside.

Murmuring secrets, soft and low,
In the drift, we let go.
With every breath, we find our way,
In the fog, we choose to stay.

The Language of Dampened Leaves

Whispers of the forest play,
As breezes weave the wordless sway.
In every drop, a story spun,
A dance of shadows, green and fun.

Rustling tales, the branches speak,
Silent secrets, soft and meek.
Nature's breath in verdant hues,
A symphony of ancient clues.

Morning kisses gently fall,
Each leaf a note in nature's call.
A moment held, a fleeting glance,
In droplets' rhythm, we find our dance.

Beyond the bark, life intertwines,
In quiet places, beauty shines.
Beneath the canopy's embrace,
The language flows in nature's grace.

Carved in silence, voices blend,
In dampened leaves, our hearts transcend.
From root to sky, the tale takes flight,
A verdant ode to day and night.

Sighs of the Rain-Kissed Soil

Underneath the weeping sky,
The thirsty earth breathes a soft sigh.
With each drop, the world awakes,
In tender pulses, the silence breaks.

The scent of life, a sweet embrace,
Emerging life in hidden space.
Grains of promise take their form,
In every tear, the earth is warm.

Beneath the weight of memories,
The soil hums with ancient pleas.
Roots entwined in deep repose,
Weaving dreams where the water flows.

Every whisper, every breath,
In rain's embrace, we dance with death.
Yet life endures; it finds its way,
In every storm, the earth will play.

From puddle's gleam to mountain's rise,
A tale unfolds 'neath brooding skies.
Together, we grow strong and bold,
In sighs of soil, our lives unfold.

Secrets in the Celestial Cascade

Stars pixelate the night so deep,
Where dreams in silence, softly creep.
A river flows of radiant light,
Whispering secrets to the night.

Nebulae swirl, in colors bright,
Telling tales of distant flight.
In cosmic arms, we drift away,
Finding peace in starlit play.

Galaxies weave a tapestry,
Of timelessness, infinity.
In cosmic waves, our hopes take sail,
In every twinkle, we're set to trail.

Through the void, where stardust sings,
We taste the joy that living brings.
With every pulse, a heart so vast,
In celestial secrets, we are cast.

Beyond horizons, dreams ignite,
In every heartbeat of the night.
Together we find our place in space,
In the celestial cascade's embrace.

Echoes in the Glistening Gloom

In twilight's clutch, a stillness lies,
While shadows stretch towards the skies.
Each echo whispers tales untold,
In glistening gloom, the night is bold.

A gentle sigh of passing nights,
Where every heart in stillness fights.
Reflections dance on hidden streams,
As darkness cradles moonlit dreams.

In corners where the silence grows,
The past lingers, softly flows.
Each moment glows in silver pale,
As history weaves an endless trail.

Over silent hills, shadows creep,
In echoes, secrets gently seep.
A song of night, both soft and grand,
In glistening gloom, together we stand.

The world beneath the stars aligns,
In echoed breaths, the heart entwines.
Through quiet paths, our spirits roam,
In the night's embrace, we find our home.

Invisible Threads of Water's Whisper

In the quiet of the stream,
Threads of water weave a dream,
Catch the shimmer, soft and light,
Whispered secrets take their flight.

Dancing droplets on the skin,
Echoes of the world within,
Gentle ripples, soft and low,
Nature's song, a fluid flow.

Beneath the willows, shadows play,
As the water glides away,
Invisible threads tie us tight,
Binding hearts in soft twilight.

Listen close, the ripples sigh,
Beneath the vast and endless sky,
Water's voice, a soothing balm,
In its embrace, the world is calm.

Woven tales of earth and stream,
In the twilight, softly gleam,
Invisible threads in moonlight's glow,
Whispering dreams we long to know.

Dreams Drenched in Celestial Light

In the stillness of the night,
Dreams emerge in fading light,
Stars in whispers, softly call,
Celestial visions, rise and fall.

Guided by the moon's embrace,
Chasing shadows, we find grace,
In the depths of silent skies,
Hope ignites, and softly flies.

Colors blend in cosmic streams,
Painting paths through woven dreams,
Galaxies swirl, and hearts ignite,
Drenched in glow, all feels so right.

Every twinkle, every spark,
Leading us from dark to dark,
With each breath, we reach the height,
Touched by dreams, drenched in light.

In the dawn, the visions fade,
Yet the memories, never stayed,
Celestial whispers, forever bright,
Guiding us into the light.

Hushed Reverie of the Morning Shower

Gentle rhythm, soft and clear,
Morning droplets, all draw near,
Hushed reverie begins to play,
Washing night away, away.

Steam and fragrance fill the air,
Moments linger, free from care,
As the world begins to wake,
Softly waking dreams we make.

Sunbeams dance on tender skin,
Cleansing all the doubts within,
In this sanctuary of light,
Morning whispers feel so right.

Every droplet, pure and free,
Shelter us in harmony,
Hushed embrace, a fleeting hour,
Cocooned in morning's gentle shower.

As the day begins to rise,
Carried forth on new sunrise,
Nature's gift, in water's flow,
Hushed reverie, forever glow.

The Soft Pulse of Rain-Kissed Night

Moonlight shimmers on the ground,
In the stillness, peace is found,
Raindrops murmur, soft and light,
Whispers dance in mirrored night.

Each drop sings a lullaby,
As the stars begin to sigh,
The earth breathes with every sound,
In this magic, all is bound.

Pavements glisten, darkened hue,
Embrace the night, soaked and true,
Lonely clouds drift, dreams take flight,
Underneath the rain-kissed night.

Echoes of the world below,
Travel gently where winds blow,
In this moment, time feels right,
The soft pulse of pure delight.

Wrapped in nature's tender care,
Hearts set free in cool, fresh air,
In the rhythm, secrets ignite,
Lost in love, the rain-kissed night.

The Tapestry of Falling Echoes

In shadows where dreams dance,
Threads of whispers entwine.
Beneath the veil of silence,
Fading echoes softly pine.

Each note a forgotten tale,
Woven in twilight's grace.
Fragments of lost wishes,
Adrift in time and space.

The loom of night unravels,
Starlit paths unfurl.
As twilight gently falls,
Secrets begin to swirl.

In the heart of the weave,
Memories pulse and breathe.
Every stitch a heartbeat,
In the fabric of belief.

A tapestry of shadows,
Where light and dark collude.
Whispers stitch the silence,
A dance of solitude.

Hidden Wishes Under the Rain's Touch

Raindrops like whispers fall,
Kissing the earth below.
Each drop carries a wish,
In the twilight's glow.

Beneath the cloudy shroud,
Dreams begin to rise.
Hopes wrapped in silver trails,
Under weeping skies.

The puddles hold secrets,
Mirrors of the heart.
Reflecting all our longings,
In every tiny part.

As the storm softens,
Wishes take flight.
Carried by the breeze,
Into the night.

Hidden in the raindrops,
Lies the pulse of fate.
Each splash a promise,
In time, they'll cultivate.

Whispers of Evermore in the Storm

Amidst the roaring thunder,
Soft whispers rise anew.
In the heart of the tempest,
Dreams find their way through.

Lightning etches stories,
Across the darkened skies.
Each flash a fleeting moment,
Where the soul truly flies.

The wind carries secrets,
Through branches bare and bold.
In the storm's fierce grip,
A tapestry unfolds.

With every drop that falls,
Echoes fill the air.
The symphony of silence,
In the world laid bare.

Whispers of evermore,
Linger in the night.
In the eye of the storm,
Hope hides in plain sight.

Glistening Storylines in Searing Haze

Heat waves shimmer softly,
Stories flutter and sway.
In the dance of the sunlight,
Truths become the play.

Under the searing sky,
Life paints in golden hues.
Each storyline glistens,
With colors rich and true.

The earth exhales its tales,
In whispers, warm and deep.
While memories shimmer bright,
In the silence, they seep.

Beneath the day's embrace,
The heart finds its refrain.
In glistening storylines,
Beauty hides in pain.

With every breath of warmth,
Hope emerges to rise.
In the haze of the heat,
Life dares to mesmerize.

Beneath Drenched Delights of Dawn

In the glow of morning light,
Petals glisten with the dew,
Whispers of the night take flight,
Nature breathes a gentle hue.

Birds awaken, soft and bright,
Songs of joy begin to swell,
Beneath the softening sight,
Hope is woven in the bell.

Branches sway with tender grace,
Sunrise paints the sky in gold,
Time unfolds in warm embrace,
Every moment to behold.

Clouds disperse in cotton white,
As the world starts to ignite,
Colors blend in soft daylight,
Drenched in love, the heart is light.

With each breath, the day begins,
Laughter dances in the air,
Life returns, and soft, it spins,
Beneath dawn's delights laid bare.

A Symphony of Soft Showers

Gentle drops on windowpanes,
Nature's song begins to play,
Each note falls like sweet refrains,
In a warm and tender sway.

Rhythms echo, hearts align,
Pattering on the thirsty ground,
In a world both soft and fine,
Harmony in water found.

Lush green blooms begin to rise,
Painting landscapes fresh and new,
Underneath the moody skies,
All is kissed in nature's dew.

As the breezes start to blow,
Rustling leaves begin to dance,
In this symphony, we flow,
Lost in raindrops' sweet romance.

Every droplet, a soft voice,
Telling tales of love and grace,
In the rain, we all rejoice,
Finding beauty in this space.

Murmurs of the Fleeting Breeze

Through the trees, a soft voice glides,
Whispers secrets, fleeting flight,
Carried on the gentle tides,
Of a day that turns to night.

Across the hills, it bends and sways,
Brushing past in subtle play,
Echoes of the sunlit days,
Fading softly, drift away.

Warm and cool, a change of scene,
Tickling leaves with playful hands,
In the space where dreams have been,
Carrying the world's demands.

Moments pass, like grains of sand,
In its grasp, the soul finds peace,
Grateful hearts will understand,
With the breeze, we find release.

Unseen magic in the air,
Murmurs weave a tale untold,
In the quiet, everywhere,
Fleeting dreams start to unfold.

The Dance of Raindrop Secrets

Raindrops twirl in graceful spins,
On the rooftops, they cascade,
In their dance, the silence thins,
Each a story, softly laid.

Puddles form, reflecting light,
Mirroring the sky above,
In the rhythm of the night,
Each drop sings of life and love.

Little sparks of joy descend,
Painting paths on streets so bare,
With each splash, the worries mend,
Carried off in soft, cool air.

Beneath the clouds, a world anew,
In the rainfall's gentle sway,
Secrets spilled from skies of blue,
Telling tales in rich ballet.

As the storm begins to fade,
Nature twirls in sweet delight,
In the dance of dreams remade,
Raindrops hug the earth goodnight.

Hidden Melodies of the Rainfall

In whispers soft, the raindrops fall,
Each one a note, a gentle call.
They dance on rooftops, a sweet refrain,
Melodies hidden in the falling rain.

With every splash, the earth awakes,
As puddles form in gentle lakes.
Nature sings in rhythmic hue,
A symphony made fresh and new.

Beneath the clouds, a canvas gray,
Yet every drop will find a way.
To paint a song upon the ground,
A melody that knows no bound.

Listen closely, hear the sound,
Of life renewed from solid ground.
In hidden rhythms, hearts find peace,
As rain brings forth a sweet release.

So let the storm play on its stage,
As nature writes its timeless page.
For in the rain, our souls will soar,
To hidden melodies forevermore.

Soft Voices in the Storm's Embrace

The storm arrives with whispers low,
Its voice a tremor, a gentle flow.
Each gust of wind, a cautious plea,
Soft voices call from sea to sea.

Within the thunder, secrets thrive,
In every flash, the shadows dive.
The sky unfolds a mystic tune,
As raindrops paint the silver moon.

Embraced by clouds, the world takes flight,
In storm's embrace, we find our light.
A symphony of wild delight,
Where chaos spins to pure insight.

With every heartbeat, nature sings,
Of passion borne from stormy things.
Soft voices rise in rhythmic form,
To cradle dreams within the storm.

Let the thunder roll, let it sing,
For in the dark, our hopes take wing.
Embrace the voices loud and clear,
As stormy nights draw us near.

Serenade of the Pattering Drops

A serenade in twilight's grace,
The drops patter down, a soft embrace.
Each splash a word, a heart's reply,
A symphony beneath the sigh.

Like tiny dancers on the ground,
In harmony, their joy is found.
As shadows stretch and colors blend,
The evening sings, the world transcends.

Much like a kiss, the rains appear,
To wash away the weight of fear.
They beckon dreams to rise and play,
In rhythm with the fading day.

Their whispered notes weave tales so bright,
Of hopes and wishes in the night.
And with each drop that falls anew,
The world awakens, deep and true.

Let every patter guide the heart,
As raindrops share their sacred art.
In serenades of soft romance,
The fleeting moments dance and prance.

Shadows Playing in the Liquid Light

In liquid light, the shadows play,
A dance of dreams that drift away.
Each droplet holds a story told,
Reflections shimmer, soft and bold.

Amidst the rain, the colors gleam,
A world awash in nature's dream.
The echoes whisper through the night,
As shadows weave in liquid light.

They blend and swirl, a canvas vast,
Each fleeting moment, gone so fast.
Yet in their wake, they leave a trace,
Of beauty carved in time and space.

The drumming rain, a heartbeat near,
It calls the shadows, drawing near.
And in their dance, the world aligns,
With every drop, a new design.

So let them whirl, let them fly,
In liquid light, beneath the sky.
For in that play, we find the key,
To shadows' songs that set us free.

Visions Merging with the Mist

In the early dawn's glow,
A tapestry unfolds,
Shapes entwined in fog's embrace,
Whispers of the untold.

Silhouettes dance with ease,
Their secrets softly blend,
Nature's breath a silent sigh,
Where moments never end.

Colors fade to gray,
Yet beauty lingers there,
Every path a mystery,
Woven in the air.

Softly, shadows beckon,
As time begins to bend,
In the merging of the world,
New dreams rise and descend.

Echoing Silence in the Silver Splendor

Moonlight drapes the landscape,
In shimmering attire,
Each sparkle holds a secret,
Every twinkle, a desire.

Waves of quietude roll,
In the midnight's embrace,
Silence sings a melody,
Crafting time and space.

Stars reflect on water,
Like diamonds in the deep,
Echoing the stillness,
Singing dreams we keep.

In shadows and in light,
We wander through the night,
In silver's soft embrace,
We drift out of sight.

The Gentle Caress of Precipitation's Art

Raindrops kiss the pavement,
With laughter in their fall,
Nature's soft caress,
Whispers like a call.

Each droplet paints a story,
On rooftops, trees and ground,
A symphony of water,
In harmony, unbound.

Puddles mirror worlds,
Reflecting skies of gray,
In each ripple, a dance,
Of life's sweet ballet.

Beneath the stormy sky,
Organic brushstrokes blend,
The gentle art of rain,
Where earth and heaven mend.

Night Sounds Wrapped in Water's Embrace

Rippling waters murmur,
In the quiet night air,
Soft echoes of the dark,
Bathe the world, laid bare.

Crickets sing a lullaby,
Underneath the stars,
While flowing streams compose,
A symphony from afar.

The world, cloaked in shadows,
In twilight's soft decree,
Every whispering current,
Brings serenity.

Wrapped in water's embrace,
The night unfolds its dreams,
As nature hums in chorus,
By the moon's silver beams.

Cadence of Heartbeats in the Storm

In the night, the thunder calls,
Rhythms pulse through weathered walls.
Lightning paints the darkened sky,
Hearts beat fast, as storms draw nigh.

Raindrops whisper secrets sweet,
Tales of love and longing meet.
Together we embrace the night,
In the tempest, holding tight.

Echoes dance on winds of change,
Roots of passion rearrange.
Every heartbeat, fierce and bold,
Like the stories yet untold.

Through the chaos, we find grace,
In each storm, we find our place.
Cadence softens all the fears,
With each pulse, we count the years.

So let the fury rage outside,
In our haven, love won't hide.
As the storm begins to calm,
Feel our hearts, a soothing balm.

Dreamscapes Woven in the Rain's Embrace

In twilight's glow, the raindrops fall,
Painting dreams upon the wall.
Softly wrapped in misty hues,
Woven tales, where hope renews.

Each droplet brings a whispered thought,
A world of wonder gently caught.
Through the rain's tender caress,
We find solace, sweet success.

Clouds meander, secrets spun,
In the morn, the chasing sun.
We sip on dreams like morning tea,
Floating high, wild and free.

In puddles deep, reflections play,
Mirrored hopes come out to sway.
Every splash, a laugh, a sigh,
In rain's embrace, we learn to fly.

So dance beneath the silver streams,
Catch the echoes of our dreams.
In this world, where rain will fall,
Love's the thread, encompassing all.

Flickers of Inspiration Through the Mist

In the haze, a spark ignites,
Whispered words take graceful flights.
Ideas dance like fireflies,
Illuminating darkened skies.

Through the mist, a voice calls clear,
Promises of visions near.
Each flicker brings a chance to see,
The endless depths of artistry.

Inspiration flows like streams,
Awakening forgotten dreams.
From the fog, new paths arise,
Painting stories, bold and wise.

As the world shifts, blurred and bright,
We grasp these visions, hold them tight.
Every breath, a spark to share,
Crafting wisdom through the air.

So let the mist envelop you,
Embrace the visions that feel true.
In every flicker, life expands,
A tapestry from gentle hands.

Enigmas Caught in the Rain's Dance

In shadows cast by falling rain,
Mysteries swirl in the refrain.
Footsteps echo, lost in time,
Searching for a hidden rhyme.

Raindrops whisper tales untold,
Secrets wrapped in shimmers gold.
Every splash a question waits,
A puzzle sealed by nature's gates.

With each drop, the world transforms,
Color and form in wild swarms.
In this dance, we spin and sway,
Finding magic in the gray.

Clarity flickers, then withdraws,
In the tempest, nature draws.
Every enigma, bound to tease,
Hidden truths in gusty breeze.

So sway within the rain's embrace,
Discover fragments of your place.
In each riddle that you face,
Find the beauty in the chase.

Quiet Revelations in Falling Memory

Whispers softly in the night,
Echoes of a dream in flight,
Colors blend in fading light,
Memories drift, a gentle sight.

Each moment flows like quiet streams,
Catching fragments of our dreams,
In the stillness, silence beams,
Unraveled seams of time's regimes.

Shadows dance upon the ground,
With each breath, a truth is found,
Lost in thoughts that swirl around,
A tapestry of past unbound.

We ponder paths we could have walked,
In whispered tones, our spirits talked,
Underneath the stars, we flocked,
Through distant skies, our hearts unlocked.

In twilight's hue, the silence lies,
As fading light begins to rise,
Embrace the hush, hear all the sighs,
For in the stillness, wisdom flies.

Ephemeral Tales in the Pouring Dusk

Rain descends in gentle drops,
Telling stories, time just stops,
Whispers fade as daylight flops,
In twilight's kiss, the heart just hops.

Fragments dance in puddles formed,
Reflections bright, emotions warmed,
In every splash, the past is scorned,
Ephemeral dreams, no hope's adorned.

Each heartbeat syncs with nature's flow,
Moments shared, both fast and slow,
Through smoky mist, our secrets grow,
In pouring dusk, the memories glow.

Caught in limbo, the world spins round,
In stories lost, yet still profound,
Together hand in hand, we're bound,
As dusk pours forth a dreamy sound.

Evanescent tales we weave and weave,
Whispers linger; do not grieve,
In the rain, we learn to believe,
For in each drop, life finds reprieve.

The Heartbeat of Raindrop Reflections

Raindrops fall, a rhythmic beat,
Nature's song beneath our feet,
Every splash, a pulse, a treat,
In this dance, our hearts repeat.

Mirrored skies in puddles lie,
Echoes of the clouds nearby,
In silence, thoughts begin to fly,
Raindrop whispers, tender sigh.

Beneath gray clouds, a hidden glow,
Softly flowing, currents slow,
In the rain's embrace, we grow,
Heartbeat quickens as we flow.

Every droplet carries dreams,
Memories caught in silver streams,
In fleeting moments, nothing seems,
As nature croons with gentle themes.

The world awash in liquid light,
In raindrop dances, pure delight,
A heartbeat found in the night,
Reflections gleam, the heart takes flight.

The Celestial Caress of Water's Soliloquy

Gentle streams and rippling waves,
Softly sing as silence paves,
In nature's arms, our spirit braves,
A tranquil mind, the heart it saves.

The moonlight paints the water bright,
Carried whispers, pure and light,
As stars unlock the velvet night,
A soothing touch, in dreams, we flight.

In water's voice, we find our peace,
Melodies that never cease,
A symphony that brings release,
A sacred bond, a calm increase.

Echoing through the tranquil blue,
Each wave a story, old yet new,
In ripples soft, our fears undo,
The soul unveiled, horizons true.

As rivers flow to oceans vast,
Time dissolves where futures passed,
In water's caress, we are cast,
In silent dreams, our hearts amassed.

Lullabies of the Gentle Storm

Soft whispers weave through night,
A melody in silver light.
Clouds caress the slumbering sky,
As dreams and raindrops gently sigh.

Every droplet sings a tune,
Beneath the watchful waning moon.
Nature hums in tranquil grace,
A soothing balm, a warm embrace.

The trees sway lightly in the breeze,
Dancing softly with such ease.
In this hush, our hearts take flight,
Cradled in the storm's delight.

Curtains drawn, the world outside,
In the rhythm, we can abide.
As lullabies begin to soar,
We drift away to nevermore.

Sweet slumber calls, let go the day,
In the gentle storm, we'll stay.
Wrapped in dreams, we softly roam,
In lullabies, we find our home.

Unseen Voices in the Downpour

In the cloak of heavy rain,
Whispers echo, soft and plain.
Voices dance on puddled ground,
Solace found, where peace is crowned.

Threads of water weave their song,
In the dark, we all belong.
Unseen hearts in each downpour,
Resonate like waves to shore.

Nature speaks in hushed refrain,
Bringing solace through the pain.
Lost in thought, we hear their call,
Tender secrets, love for all.

The night unfolds with gentle grace,
Each droplet drawn, a warm embrace.
Memories hidden in each stream,
Unseen voices weave our dream.

Beneath the sky's majestic dome,
In the downpour, we find home.
Voices rise in rhythmic flow,
In the rain, our spirits grow.

Serene Shadows of the Rain

Shadows play on streets so bare,
Whispered tales hang in the air.
Each drop a brush of silver hue,
Painting life, transforming view.

Silent moments wrapped in grey,
Serenity led astray.
Clouds weave softly overhead,
Cradling dreams in twilight's thread.

Rippling rivers, glistening light,
Reflect the magic of the night.
Shadows dance in rhythmic sway,
Guided softly by the spray.

In the dusk, we find our peace,
With the rain, all worries cease.
Nature's pulse begins to thrum,
In the night, the quiet hum.

On this canvas, hearts align,
In shadows cast, our souls entwine.
Serene breaths through falling rain,
In this stillness, love will reign.

Twilight Serenades in the Shower

Twilight whispers soft and sweet,
As raindrops fall in quick retreat.
Melodies beneath the sky,
A serenade as night draws nigh.

Each splash sings a tender song,
In the shower where we belong.
Reflections dance in golden light,
Washing worries into night.

Gentle rhythms pulse and flow,
In the hush, our spirits glow.
Voices blend with water's grace,
Serenades in this sacred space.

Lost in time, the moments pass,
Through the shower's melting glass.
Twilight casts a spell so fine,
We find warmth, your hand in mine.

In this haven, dreams take flight,
Twilight serenades ignite.
With each drop, we rise and sing,
Together sweet, in joy we cling.

Flickers of Light in the Steady Pour

In the dark, a glimmer shines,
Raindrops dance on silent pines.
Each flash a whisper, soft and bright,
Guiding souls through the quiet night.

The world around, a curtain blurred,
Yet in stillness, a voice is heard.
Hope emerges in every bead,
Planting a dream, a vital seed.

Through torrents deep, where shadows creep,
Flickers of truth, awake from sleep.
They weave a path through stormy gloom,
Illuminating all that's doomed.

Laughter ripples, fleeting spark,
Joy ignites within the dark.
Braving currents, hearts align,
In the storm, our fates entwine.

With every drop, a tale is spun,
In the glow, we come undone.
Forging strength, we find our might,
Flickers of hope in steady night.

Traces of Breath in the Falling Mist

In the hush, a secret sigh,
Breath of earth beneath the sky.
Fog wraps round with soft embrace,
Time dissolves in this sacred space.

Each inhaled dream, a fleeting thought,
Whispers of what time forgot.
In the grey, the world stands still,
Echoes linger, as if to thrill.

Glimmers hide in droplets shy,
Softened edges where shadows lie.
A tapestry of vague design,
In the mist, our souls entwine.

Memories drift like fleeting smoke,
In silence, every heart awoke.
Breath of history intertwines,
In the stillness, truth divines.

We dance in grace, lost but found,
With every gust, love's voice resounds.
Traces linger, soft and light,
As we breathe in the falling night.

The Scent of Tales Yet Untold

In the breeze, secrets unfold,
Scent of stories yet untold.
Whispers mingle with the air,
Carrying dreams beyond compare.

Each footstep on this ancient ground,
Echoes of life in silence found.
Petals drift, a fragrant trail,
Leading us where hearts prevail.

Beneath the stars, in soft twilight,
Weaving magic, day turns night.
In the dusk, the world lays bare,
Unveiling truths that drift in air.

With every breath, new paths arise,
Hidden wonders in moonlit skies.
The scent of hope, a fleeting dream,
Flows through us like a silver stream.

Together we chase the tales of old,
Through stories written, joys unfold.
In the weave of twilight's gold,
The scent lingers, brave and bold.

Enigmas in the Veil of Raindrops

Raindrops fall, a soft embrace,
Enigmas dance in every space.
Secrets drench the earth anew,
In swirling mist, we find our view.

Whispers run where puddles lie,
Reflections mirror the cloudy sky.
Each droplet holds a fleeting guess,
A puzzle wrapped in nature's dress.

Beneath the veil, mysteries sleep,
Guarding thoughts we wish to keep.
A tapestry of water's grace,
In every splash, a hidden face.

With every storm, we seek the truth,
In playful drops, the eyes of youth.
Unraveled thoughts like thread unspool,
In the rain, we find the cool.

Enigmas linger, soft and light,
Underneath the cloak of night.
In nature's pulse, we feel the beat,
Unveiling wonders in the street.

Portals Opened by the Storm

Rumbling skies, the tempest roars,
Dark clouds dance on distant shores.
Windswept dreams take wing and soar,
As portals open, evermore.

Lightning sizzles in the night,
Casting shadows, flickering light.
Echoes of a crazed delight,
Reveal the truth beyond our sight.

Raindrops fall like whispered sighs,
Each one holding unspoken ties.
They shatter silence, cause goodbyes,
In chaos, serenity lies.

The world transforms with each breath,
In tempest's heart, we confront death.
Yet life persists, defying rest,
In storm's embrace, we're truly blessed.

So dance beneath the virtual sky,
Let lightning flash and currents fly.
For when the storm has passed us by,
New paths arise where wonders lie.

The Quietude of Damp Horizons

Gentle mist hangs low and wide,
Softening edges where dreams reside.
In muted hues, the world abides,
A calm embrace where hope confides.

Dampened earth, a fragrant breath,
Each droplet whispers life from death.
In stillness, we find our steps,
As silence wraps us in its depths.

Horizons blur in grey embrace,
Time dissolves without a trace.
The heart finds solace in this space,
Collecting shadows, every grace.

Faraway echoes softly fade,
As twilight weaves a cool cascade.
The quietude, a serenade,
Inviting peace, no debts to trade.

In moments brief, but deeply felt,
Where heavy hearts begin to melt,
We dwell in dreams, our worries spelt,
In damp horizons, love is dealt.

Luminous Threads of a Forgotten Rain

Beneath the dusk, soft echoes play,
Luminous threads in bright array.
A distant past calls, comes what may,
In whispered winds, we lose our way.

Forgotten rains, with diamonds spun,
Mark paths we walked, now overrun.
Each droplet's song, once lost, now won,
In tender light, the night begun.

Memories shimmer like silver streams,
Carried on sighs and fragile dreams.
In faded colors, time redeems,
Bound by the heart, or so it seems.

Cascading whispers from the skies,
We search for truth in veiled replies.
In twilight's glow, our spirit flies,
To capture love, where silence lies.

Oh, let us dance in that sweet glow,
Embrace the past as waters flow.
For in such threads, all hearts shall know,
Forgotten rain helps us to grow.

Mists of Memory Linger Sweetly

Mists of memory softly creep,
Nestled in dreams, where shadows weep.
Fragments of time in silence seep,
Awakening treasures we keep.

The past a breeze, a tender sigh,
Brings laughter, tears, the whispered why.
In every glance, a piece to try,
To hold the moments that go by.

Each heartbeat echoes a distant song,
A haunting tune that feels so wrong.
Yet in the mists, we still belong,
As time unfolds, we carry on.

Sweet nostalgia paints the night,
In hues of gold and fading light.
As memories blend with starlit sight,
They guide our souls, take flight, take flight.

So linger long in sweet embrace,
For in the mists, we find our place.
In every breath, a gentle trace,
Of love that time cannot erase.

Shadows Beneath Celestial Tears

In twilight's grasp, the shadows creep,
Beneath the tears that silence weep.
Whispers soft as nightingales,
Drift through darkened, endless trails.

Stars flicker, memories collide,
In the glow where secrets hide.
A dance of light in fading air,
Shadows weave without a care.

Lonely hearts in twilight fade,
Underneath the sky's cool shade.
Dreamers search for fleeting signs,
In the dusk where silence twines.

Promises in darkness bloom,
Bathed in silver, breaking gloom.
Each celestial tear a spark,
Guiding souls along the dark.

Together they find solace near,
Beneath the skies that often sneer.
In shadows deep, they shall remain,
Bound in love midst joy and pain.

The Soft Rhythm of Soaked Earth

Sinking steps on sodden ground,
In rhythm where soft echoes sound.
Each droplet's dance, a gentle sigh,
    Awakening the earth nearby.

Waves of warmth in earthy clots,
Life springing forth in tender thoughts.
    Textures rich beneath the rain,
    Holding stories, joy, and pain.

A symphony of blades and blooms,
Resilient through the springtime's tombs.
    Nature's heart beats strong and free,
    In tender hush, you'll hear its plea.

With every step, the darkness fades,
As sun peeks through the forest blades.
The earth will rise, renewed and whole,
    In soaked embrace, it finds its soul.

Time pauses on this hallowed ground,
    As beauty and life are found.
    The soft rhythm, a loving play,
Guides us through each passing day.

Dreams Wrapped in a Glistening Veil

Beneath a sky of twilight hues,
Drift softly, whispering muse.
Dreams unfold in silk and lace,
Wrapped in magic's soft embrace.

Stars weave tales of nights long past,
In glimmering threads, they are cast.
Each vision glows with pure delight,
Guiding lost souls through the night.

Fleeting moments gently sway,
Like shadows drifting into gray.
As dawn arrives with whispered grace,
Dreams retreat, yet hold their space.

Every heartbeat sings a song,
Of a tale where we belong.
Wrapped in light, we softly dream,
Of a world that sparkles and gleams.

In a veil that glistens bright,
We find solace through the night.
Though dreams may fade with morning's veil,
Their whispers linger, soft and pale.

Conversations with the Pattering Sky

In the hush where raindrops speak,
The sky converses, soft and meek.
Pattering gently on the ground,
Whispers of love in every sound.

Clouds gather, tales of distant lands,
Traveling lightly, hand in hands.
Each drop a story, rich and free,
Mingling with the earth's decree.

Songs of rain in twilight's glow,
Caressing hearts, soft and slow.
In this dance of sky and earth,
A celebration of rebirth.

Silvery tears fall like a dream,
Painting the world in a gentle scheme.
Nature listens, in silence we sigh,
In sweet communion with the sky.

Morning breaks, the patter fades,
Yet in our hearts, the magic wades.
Conversations linger on the breeze,
In every drop, life finds its peace.

Lunar Secrets Swirling in Raindrops

In moonlit dreams, soft voices sigh,
Raindrops whisper from the sky.
Secrets held in each silver bead,
A dance of wishes, a silent creed.

Beneath the glow, shadows embark,
Ripples shimmering in the dark.
They weave a tale, a gentle flight,
Awakening hearts in the quiet night.

Glistening tears on petals rest,
Holding stories, secrets confessed.
The world transforms in this embrace,
As night unveils its hidden grace.

Each drop a moment, fleeting and bright,
Carrying echoes of soft delight.
Lunar secrets swirl and play,
In the gentle raindrops' sway.

And when the dawn breaks, light will bloom,
Chasing away the night's cool gloom.
Yet in our hearts, those whispers stay,
Lunar secrets in rain's ballet.

The Waltz of Wind and Water

Wind takes flight, a playful breeze,
Caressing leaves and dancing trees.
Water joins in, a flowing song,
Together they sway, forever strong.

Rippling currents, a graceful glide,
Whispers of nature in every stride.
The earth holds fast, a tender hand,
As elements twirl across the land.

Clouds drift by, a soft parade,
In the waltz of nature, none are afraid.
Every ripple, every gust,
A reminder of beauty, pure and just.

They intertwine in a joyous embrace,
Creating rhythms, a timeless space.
With every gust and every wave,
Life's cherished moments, they engrave.

So let us dance in this harmony,
Where wind and water set us free.
In the symphony of earth and sky,
We find our spirit soaring high.

Breathing Life Under Rain's Cloak

Under the cloak of a rainy veil,
Life awakens, a whispered tale.
Each droplet nurtures, each patter sings,
A symphony of growth that nature brings.

The earth drinks deep, a thirst it knows,
As colors flourish, the garden glows.
In puddles formed, reflections play,
Imagination dances, come what may.

Raindrops fall like fleeting dreams,
They sparkle bright in silver streams.
Underneath the cover, life expands,
Planting hope in our gentle hands.

Every storm has a purpose, true,
To cleanse the heart and renew the view.
In every sigh of thunder's roar,
Lies the promise of joy in store.

So breathe life in, let the rain unfold,
Embrace the stories yet untold.
For under this cloak, we find our place,
In every droplet, in nature's grace.

Everlasting Dreams in Drenched Palettes

Drenched palettes paint the morning bright,
Colors merge in a dazzling light.
A canvas sprung from gentle rains,
Everlasting dreams in vibrant stains.

Clouds, like brushes, sweep the sky,
Creating wonders as they float by.
Every hue a tale anew,
Nature's masterpiece, pure and true.

In puddles deep, reflections flow,
Captured fragments of sunlit glow.
Every drop a moment preserved,
In this world where beauty's served.

The scent of earth, the taste of air,
Awakening spirits, beyond compare.
In drizzled colors, hope is found,
Rooted deeply in sacred ground.

So let the rain kiss dreams awake,
As every brushstroke we create.
With hearts wide open, imagination beams,
In everlasting dreams, we find our seams.

Reflections in the Glowing Puddle

In silence, the stars weep bright,
Over puddles, their soft, pale light.
Rippling whispers, secrets unfold,
Mirroring dreams, tender and bold.

The moon dips low, a silvery crest,
A cradle of dreams where shadows rest.
Each drop a tale, a moment caught,
In the stillness, wonder is sought.

Beneath the surface, memories flow,
Ebbing softly, quiet and slow.
In golden hues, reflections play,
Guiding the heart, lighting the way.

Gentle breezes stir the night air,
Carrying echoes of love and care.
With every ripple, a promise blooms,
In this puddle, hope gently looms.

So linger here, where dreams reside,
In glowing waters, let fate collide.
Each reflection, a story to share,
In the beauty found, we lay bare.

Rain-kissed Dreams of Wandering Souls

Under clouds, the world breathes deep,
Heartbeats echo where shadows creep.
A dance of raindrops on battered paths,
Painting the earth in joyous swaths.

Wandering souls in the fleeting light,
Carried gently through the endless night.
Each step whispers of journeys gone,
In rain-kissed dreams, we're never alone.

Hope alights on the wings of the breeze,
A symphony found among whispering trees.
With every storm comes a chance to renew,
In the heart of the rain, find what is true.

Beneath the downpour, laughter rings clear,
Cleansing sorrows, washing away fear.
The world awakens, vibrant and bold,
In dreams of wanderers, stories unfold.

So dance in the rain, let your spirit soar,
Embrace the wild, seek evermore.
For every drop holds a wish untold,
In rain-kissed dreams, our hearts are consoled.

Traces of Light in the Stormy Veil

A tempest brews in the night sky,
The winds howl, and the shadows sigh.
Yet amidst the chaos, sparks ignite,
Whispers of hope in the fading light.

Clouds collide with thunder's might,
Yet glimmers persist, a daring sight.
The dance of lightning, flickers and fades,
Outlining the fears that hope invades.

In the heart of storms, resilience grows,
In torrents of rain, the river flows.
Traces of light break through the grey,
Shattering darkness, leading the way.

With every flash, a vision appears,
A tapestry woven of joy and fears.
Stormy veils hide the strength below,
In trials endured, our spirits will grow.

So embrace the tempest, let thunder ring,
For after the storm, a new day will spring.
Traces of light, like diamonds gleam,
In the shadowed veil, we find our dream.

Faces of the Night Beneath the Cascade

Amidst the whispers of the falling stream,
The night enfolds in a timeless dream.
Faces of shadows in the moon's embrace,
Dancing softly in a tranquil space.

Caught in the flow of silvery tides,
Where secrets linger and mystery hides.
The echoes of laughter, a gentle breeze,
In the heart of the night, we wander with ease.

Flowing water, carrying tales of old,
Each face of the night, a spark to behold.
Beneath the cascade, stories combine,
In the lull of the night, the stars align.

Eyes alight with passion's glow,
In the embrace of darkness, we let go.
Faces in stillness, lost in the sound,
In the night's quiet gaze, unity found.

So let the night wrap you in its shroud,
In the presence of whispers, gentle and loud.
For beneath the cascade, life will unfold,
In the faces of night, our souls are bold.

Whispers through Water's Embrace

Soft ripples dance on the lake,
Carrying secrets of the night.
Moonlight shimmers, water's wake,
In gentle waves, dreams take flight.

With each whisper, tales unfold,
Of lovers lost and hope reborn.
Nature's voice, a story told,
In the quiet, beauty's sworn.

The breeze caresses, oh so light,
Stirring memories deep and vast.
In shadows cast by fading light,
Echoes linger, holding fast.

Beneath the surface, treasures hide,
In the depths, reflections play.
Locks of silver, secrets tied,
In water's arms, they softly sway.

Whispers rise with morning's breath,
As sunbeams kiss the tranquil stream.
In water's embrace, life meets death,
And in those dreams, we dare to dream.

Glimmers Against the Dusk

Amber hues streak the sky,
Painting evening's gentle caress.
Stars awaken, time slips by,
In the silence, dreams express.

Shadows stretch and softly lean,
Curtains drawn on day's embrace.
Whispers glide, serene, unseen,
As night unfolds with tender grace.

The horizon holds a spark,
A fleeting glimpse of hope anew.
In the twilight's beckoning dark,
Every glimmer, a promise true.

With each moment, stillness grows,
Nature hums its final tune.
Underneath the moonlight's glow,
Hearts unite beneath a rune.

As dusk envelops, secrets sigh,
In a world that slows its pace.
Glimmers fade, but still we fly,
Into the night, our dreams embrace.

Reflections in a Dewy Mirage

Morning breathes with misty grace,
Dewdrops glisten on the grass.
Nature's mirror, a tranquil place,
Reflects the moment as it passes.

Colors burst in softest beams,
Mystic visions come alive.
In each droplet, hidden dreams,
Emerge anew, begin to thrive.

Beneath the surface, beauty lies,
Carried gently by the dawn.
A tapestry in radiant ties,
With every sunbeam, light is drawn.

The world awakens, whispers rise,
In the silence, stories blend.
Through each sparkle, truth defies,
And as we pause, our hearts extend.

Reflections shimmer, softly fade,
Time weaves memories to adore.
In dewy mirage, dreams parade,
Eternity whispered, evermore.

Sheltering Stories of the Storm

Thunder rumbles, a tale untold,
Clouds embrace the restless sky.
Wind carries whispers, brave and bold,
In storm's embrace, hearts learn to fly.

Raindrops dance on leaves below,
Nature's rhythm, wild delight.
Through the tempest, secrets flow,
In the chaos, dreams ignite.

Sheltering skies hold sorrows deep,
A cradle for the weary souls.
In the darkness, no need to weep,
For in the storm, healing rolls.

Lightning flashes, a moment's spark,
Illuminating paths we tread.
In the heart of shadows dark,
Hope emerges, alive, not dead.

When the storm has passed away,
Stories linger in the air.
Sheltered souls in sun's soft sway,
Find the strength in love and care.

Secrets in the Silver Mist

In the dawn's quiet breath, fading light,
Secrets whisper soft, in the night.
Moonbeams dance over the silent streams,
Echoing wonders, lost in dreams.

Veils of fog embrace the hidden land,
Footsteps tread softly, hand in hand.
Ancient tales linger in the air,
Each moment savored, beyond compare.

Nature's palette, hues of gray,
Unfolding mysteries, dawn's ballet.
Soundless echoes round the bend,
Where paths of stories intertwine and blend.

Whispers of longing in the dew,
Softly curling, like the day is new.
Stars fade slowly, into the mist,
Embracing secrets, twilight kissed.

In this realm where shadows play,
All our secrets hide away.
Each drop of rain, a tale untold,
In the silent silver, brave and bold.

Echoes of a Hidden Sky

Beneath the canvas, stars reside,
Woven tales of hope and pride.
Each flicker paints the velvet night,
In a dance that feels so right.

Clouds drift softly, dreams in tow,
Journeys taken, rivers flow.
Murmurs rise; the earth will sigh,
In the shadows of the sky.

Cascades of color, twilight's hue,
Embrace the silence, crisp and true.
Every heartbeat, echo's trace,
Carried gently, time and space.

Hidden wonders awaken here,
Fragrant whispers, sweet and clear.
Nature's heartbeat, pulse-like sighs,
Caught within the hidden skies.

Echoes linger on cool winds,
Like secret promises, life begins.
Under the realm where spirits glide,
In this sanctuary, we confide.

Shimmering Hush of Falling Drops

Gentle rain weaves through the night,
Whispers softly, pure delight.
Each droplet sings a serenade,
Nature's lullaby, unafraid.

Moonlight glistens on the ground,
In the stillness, a magic found.
Shimmering hush, the world aglow,
Dancing softly, as breezes blow.

Every drop tells tales of old,
Of sunlit days and nights so bold.
Carried forth by the winds' embrace,
In tender moments, time finds grace.

The earth drinks deep, quenched and whole,
In each falling drop, life's sweet soul.
With every splash, the echoes rise,
Painting dreams across the skies.

In this soft embrace, we find our way,
Lost in rhythm, night steals the day.
Shimmering hush, let worries fade,
In the falling drops, our hearts are laid.

Beneath the Veil of Clouded Dreams

Beneath the veil of shadowed night,
Clouded dreams take gentle flight.
Fleeting echoes, sounds of grace,
Whispers lingering in this space.

Veils of twilight cloak the skies,
Where secrets breathe and silence lies.
Every star a distant friend,
Guiding those who seek to mend.

Time unfolds in muted tones,
Embracing shadows, whispering bones.
In this realm, we dance anew,
With every heartbeat, fresh and true.

Winds carry tales across the night,
Of hidden worlds, just out of sight.
Dreamers wander, souls entwined,
In a tapestry, love defined.

Beneath the veil, we find release,
In every sigh, we seek our peace.
In clouded dreams, tales of old,
Woven together, brave and bold.

Tales of the Weeping Sky

Beneath a blanket of gray,
Whispers of sorrow drift away.
Clouds gather like ancient ghosts,
In the silence, the heart's lost toast.

Raindrops dance on window panes,
Each a note from joy and pains.
They weep for stories yet untold,
Of dreams that shimmer but grow cold.

Thunder rumbles in the night,
A symphony of fading light.
Lightning flashes, fierce and bright,
Like the truth burning, out of sight.

In the quiet, voices speak,
Of the hopes that seem so bleak.
The sky weeps with every tear,
A reminder of love held dear.

So listen close, when it rains,
To the tales that wash the plains.
For in each drop, a story lies,
In the weeping of the skies.

The Soundtrack of the Swallowed Night

In the hush where shadows creep,
The night holds secrets and dreams deep.
Stars whisper in a muted glow,
Painting stories only night can know.

Crickets play a melody soft,
Notes of longing that drift aloft.
The moon hums a lullaby sweet,
Guiding hearts to a tranquil beat.

Every rustle in the trees,
Carries echoes of the breeze.
A serenade of dark unveils,
The soundtracks of our hidden trails.

Through the stillness, a sigh escapes,
Woven within the night's landscapes.
Each moment holds a breathless pause,
As music cradles our unspoken cause.

So close your eyes and drift along,
To the rhythm of the night's own song.
Let your spirit take its flight,
In the embrace of the swallowed night.

Tides of Tranquility Underneath

Waves whisper secrets in the deep,
Where tranquil souls find peace to keep.
The ocean cradles dreams so wide,
On the surface, a shifting tide.

Beneath the foam, a silent song,
Where echoing heartbeats belong.
Ripples carry tales untold,
In the depths where time is gold.

Seaweed dances with gentle grace,
In the blue embrace, we find our place.
Each current pulls, each wave a kiss,
Moments captured in watery bliss.

The horizon blushes, sunlight beams,
Shattering notions, birthing dreams.
Together we sway in soothing flow,
As tides of calm begin to grow.

So let the sea whisper in your ear,
And wash away all doubt and fear.
In its depths, tranquility reigns,
Forever tied to the ocean's veins.

Fragments of Dusk in a Rainfall

As daylight bends and softly fades,
Fragments of dusk in colors cascades.
Each drop of rain a fleeting sigh,
Painting the canvas of the sky.

Golden hues meet silver streams,
In the twilight, we weave our dreams.
The world breathes deep, a sweet embrace,
In each burst of rain, we find our place.

Shadows lengthen, the chill may bite,
Yet there's beauty in the falling light.
The air is clean, the earth awake,
Each moment precious, ours to take.

With every patter on window sills,
The heart rejoices, the spirit fills.
Fragments of laughter, memories blend,
In the showers, old wounds mend.

So dance beneath the weeping sky,
Let the fragments of dusk fly high.
In every drop, life's rhythm plays,
As we welcome the night's embrace.

The Language of Drops on Leaves

In soft whispers, the droplets speak,
Nature's rhythm, gentle and sleek.
Each leaf a canvas, a story to tell,
Of sunlit days and nights that fell.

Under the canopy, silence obeys,
As emerald shivers catch sunlight's rays.
The symphony plays with a shushing sound,
Where beauty in stillness can truly be found.

From branches high to the earth below,
They dance and tumble, a liquid flow.
In harmony spoken, in droplets they share,
The secrets of life, so vivid and rare.

When winds come calling, they sway and twirl,
A language of nature, a soft, swaying pearl.
Each drop captures moments, ephemeral grace,
A fleeting embrace, in this tranquil space.

So pause for a heartbeat, let nature unfold,
The beauty of stories in droplets of gold.
Listen to wisdom that nature bequeaths,
In the language of drops, as they fall on leaves.

Mysteries Wrapped in Moisture

Fog blankets the valley, secrets concealed,
In whispers of dew, the day is revealed.
Each droplet a gem, a story untold,
Mysteries wrapped in the soft, moist fold.

The world shimmers gently, a dreamlike mist,
Breath of the earth, in twilight kissed.
Shadowy outlines loom in the haze,
Lending the evening an ethereal gaze.

Clouds drift lazily, their burdens of rain,
Weaving together both joy and pain.
Nature holds close the answers we seek,
In the delicate dance of the damp and the meek.

In every raindrop, the universe sighs,
Reflecting the stars in the dampened skies.
Each bead carries tales of time long past,
A history written, in water amassed.

So wander through whispers, embrace the unknown,
In mysteries wrapped, let your spirit be sown.
For the magic of moisture holds lessons quite deep,
As twilight descends, into dreams we leap.

Echoing Silence of the Rainy Night.

In the hush of the night, the rain softly falls,
An echoing silence, where nature calls.
The patter of drops on a rooftop song,
Melodies linger, but time feels so long.

Streetlights shimmer through curtains of grey,
Illuminating paths where shadows play.
In puddles reflecting a world set aglow,
Lives intertwine in the dance of the flow.

The air holds a sweetness, a scent that is rare,
With each drop that lands, a moment laid bare.
A heartbeat, a whisper, a fleeting embrace,
In the echoing silence, we find our place.

The tempest may roar, yet peace we will find,
Wrapped in the solace the rain leaves behind.
As dreams slip like water, we lay down our fears,
In the echo of silence, the night disappears.

So let the rain nurture the seeds in our soul,
Each drop a reminder that makes us feel whole.
In the stillness of night, let us dance with delight,
Echoing silence, under starlit light.

Whispers of the Drizzling Night.

Under the moon's watch, soft droplets descend,
Each whisper of nature, a message to send.
The world wrapped in comfort, a blanket of grey,
As whispers of drizzle carry dreams away.

Umbrellas bloom like flowers at dusk,
Shielding the wanderers, a moment to trust.
With every soft splash, a heartbeat is heard,
In the stillness of night, the heart finds its word.

The streets shimmer gently, reflections aglow,
A canvas of splendor, where shadows ebb slow.
In puddles of silver, our hopes take flight,
Awash in the echoes of the drizzling night.

The air is enriched with a fragrant embrace,
Nature's own perfume perfuming the space.
With every soft drizzle, new stories we weave,
In whispers so tender that night will believe.

So dance in the droplets, let laughter ignite,
In the magic that lasts through the drizzling night.
For in every moment, as shadows take flight,
We find the sweet whispers, the joy of the night.

Whispers of the Drenched Twilight

In twilight's embrace, shadows dance,
Soft whispers drift, a fleeting chance.
The sky blushes deep, a violet hue,
Stars awaken, bidding day adieu.

Raindrops linger on the cool ground,
Murmurs of secrets begin to sound.
Nature holds still, a promise to keep,
In the dusk's arms, our dreams will seep.

Leaves shimmer under the fading light,
As night unfolds, the world feels right.
Hand in hand through the dampened air,
We share each thought, a bond laid bare.

Echoes of laughter, soft and low,
Rippling through the twilight's glow.
In every shimmer, a tale untold,
In whispers of twilight, hearts unfold.

The moon rises high, a guardian bright,
Casting its gaze over weary night.
In the drenched twilight, love intertwines,
Where every heartbeat eternally shines.

Secrets in the Silver Drizzle

Silver droplets fall from the sky,
Whispers of secrets drift quietly by.
The world is cloaked in a soft gray veil,
Under this drizzle, love's tales prevail.

Pavements shimmer, reflecting the light,
With each gentle fall, the world feels right.
In hidden corners, we find our grace,
Dancing in shadows, we lose our place.

The rhythm of rain sings a sweet tune,
As we walk beneath the watchful moon.
Fingers entwined, we tread softly here,
Where the drizzle whispers, love draws near.

In alleys damp with forgotten dreams,
The silver outlines of life, it seems.
Each droplet carries a message clear,
Secrets entwined, forever held dear.

And as the night deepens, we find our peace,
In the sweet silver rain, our hearts unleash.
With every forgotten story we've sown,
In this drizzle's embrace, we feel at home.

Echoes in the Shimmering Mist

In the morning's blush, mist starts to rise,
Echoes of dreams swirl beneath gray skies.
Whispers of dawn, soft and unclear,
Embrace the stillness, presence is near.

Shapes in the fog, fleeting and shy,
Carried on breezes, they fade, then fly.
With every heartbeat, the world holds its breath,
In this shimmering mist, we conquer death.

Clouds kiss the earth, a gentle caress,
Nature's embrace feels like pure finesse.
Hand in hand, we wander through time,
Lost in the echoes, our souls climb.

Laughter bubbles softly in the damp air,
As moments unfold, nothing to compare.
Every step taken leaves footprints behind,
In the mist's embrace, our hearts unwind.

As shadows lengthen, the day transforms,
In echoes of mist, our love warms.
Together forever, lost and then found,
In shimmering whispers, our hopes are bound.

Veils of Laughter in the Downpour

The downpour begins with a playful cheer,
Veils of laughter dance, drawing us near.
Splashes of joy fill the puddles around,
In the storm's embrace, magic is found.

Each raindrop falls like music's sweet song,
Marking the rhythm where we belong.
With hearts wide open, we race through the rain,
In laughter's embrace, we feel no pain.

Colors collide in a whimsical show,
As bright umbrellas bloom, the world seems aglow.
In every tempest, a story unfolds,
With laughter as armor, we find our bolds.

Under gray clouds, our spirits ignite,
In the downpour's embrace, everything feels right.
Laughter echoes loud, drowning out fears,
In this storm of joy, we wash away tears.

So let it rain fiercely; let the skies roar,
In the laughter of downpours, we seek for more.
Together we'll dance, in this wild symphony,
Where laughter and love can always roam free.

Tones of the Weeping Clouds

Clouds gather softly, weep with grace,
Whispers of sorrow fill the space.
Silver tears fall, a gentle sound,
Nature's lament, a beauty profound.

Colors of gray, blending above,
Each drop a token, a message of love.
The dreams of the sky in a hazy display,
Melodies flow as they drift away.

Through twilight's embrace, they linger and sigh,
Recall the tales of the wanderer's cry.
With each pitter-patter, they weave a new tale,
In the heart of the storm, our spirits set sail.

A song of old echoes in the air,
Life in each breath, the tender despair.
Holding the moments, as twilight grows dim,
The clouds paint our thoughts with shadows and whim.

Into the night, when all seems lost,
We find in the weeping, the life-giving cost.
For in every sorrow, a story unfolds,
In tones of the clouds, our solace beholds.

Lullabies of the Soaked Earth

Raindrops whisper on the thirsty ground,
In the hush of the night, gentle sounds abound.
Nature sings softly in damp melodies,
Cradled by earth, embraced by the trees.

Sleep now, dear soil, wrapped in the rain,
With every drop, wash away the pain.
Cocooned in silence, dreams take their flight,
Lullabies woven in the deepening night.

Fields of emerald dance, swaying slow,
Under the weight of fresh water's glow.
The scent of rebirth hangs thick in the air,
As life stirs anew, vibrant and fair.

In puddles reflecting the stars up above,
The earth holds the whispers of all that we love.
Each flicker of light speaks a lullaby,
Cradling the night as the weary wind sighs.

So let the world rest, as the earth drinks deep,
In the soothing embrace of slumber we keep.
Awake to the dawn, with a heart full of mirth,
For the night's gentle lullabies warm the soaked earth.

Hushed Stories of the Falling Sky

Falling wishes from the twilight hue,
Whispers of dreams bid the day adieu.
Storylines woven in shadows and light,
Hushed tales unfold in the calm of the night.

Each star a secret, a moment in time,
A flicker of fate in celestial rhyme.
Beneath the vast canvas of deep velvet blue,
Hearts converse softly, as the night bids adieu.

The winds carry whispers of ages past,
Echoes of lovers, their shadows cast.
In the hush of the night, they find solace here,
With stars as their witness, they hold them near.

Falling like petals from a mystical tree,
Stories unfurl in the soft symphony.
With each whispered sigh breathed into the dark,
We find in the silence, a light and a spark.

As night slowly stretches and softly descends,
The skies share their secrets with those who make amends.
In the hush of the heavens, we listen with care,
For the falling sky speaks, if we're willing to share.

The Gentle Chorus of Distant Thunder

A rumble awakens the quiet of night,
A gentle chorus, a reassuring sight.
In the depths of the storm, the heavens convene,
With whispers of thunder, a powerful sheen.

Each boom a reminder of nature's own song,
A rhythm of ages, both mighty and strong.
The heart of the tempest, it beats with bold grace,
In the dance of the storm, we find our place.

Clouds gather like storytellers, wise and old,
With tales of the earth, in their embrace, we're told.
Through intervals of silence, a magic unfolds,
In the symphony painted with blues and golds.

As flashes of light stitch the night with bright seams,
The echoes of thunder entwine with our dreams.
In nature's own concert, each heartbeat aligned,
The gentle chorus takes hold of our mind.

So listen closely, let your worries unbind,
For in distant thunder, peace you will find.
Embrace the beauty—both wild and serene,
In the laughter of storms, our souls can glean.

Delights Disguised in the Liquid Haze

In morning mist, the world awakes,
A shimmering dance on whispering lakes.
Soft echoes play where shadows blend,
Dreams concealed in a liquid trend.

Glistening droplets kiss the leaves,
A secret language the heart retrieves.
Nature's palette, bold and bright,
Delights disguised in soft twilight.

The air is rich with earthy scent,
Moments fleeting, so quickly spent.
Joy in silence, joy in space,
In the hazy veil, we find our place.

Rippling streams sing tender tunes,
Underneath the gaze of soft, bright moons.
Each wave a memory, each current a prayer,
In this liquid haze, we shed our care.

With every step, a spark ignites,
In hidden realms, where wonder excites.
Delights in disguise, forever last,
In the gentle haze of the past.

Chants of the Earth in Soaked Silence

Beneath the weight of clouds above,
The earth resounds with whispers of love.
Each raindrop's fall a hymn so pure,
In soaked silence, hearts can endure.

Roots entwine in soft embrace,
Each blade of grass a vibrant trace.
Nature's carpet, lush and wide,
In murmured tones, the earth confides.

The rivers hum their ancient song,
A melody where we belong.
Even stones are touched by fate,
In the soaked silence, we communicate.

Every puddle reflects the sky,
In stillness deep, we question why.
Chants of the earth, a sacred call,
In soaked silence, we stand tall.

In every corner, life unfolds,
Stories whispered, softly told.
Through soaked silence, we are drawn,
To the heart of nature's dawn.

Reverberations of the Clouds' Caress

Among the hills, the clouds do roam,
In their caress, we find our home.
Whispers float on gentle wind,
Reverberations where dreams rescind.

With every gust, a secret shared,
In the soft gray, we are unpaired.
Each droplet falls, a kiss, a trace,
Of longing wrapped in soft embrace.

The skyline blushes, fades to gray,
As shadows dance and drift away.
In twilight's grip, we feel the sound,
Of clouds' caress, our hearts unbound.

A symphony of soft alarms,
Nature's pulse, its open arms.
In every heartbeat, in every sigh,
Reverberations in the sky.

A tapestry of silent nights,
Crafted whispers, gentle flights.
With clouds above and dreams to chase,
We find our peace in nature's grace.

Shadowed Conversations of the Soggy Ground

Underneath the drumming rain,
The soggy ground begins to gain.
Voices rise from earth below,
In shadowed conversations, they flow.

Each puddle holds a tale so deep,
In every ripple, secrets seep.
Nature speaks through muddy tones,
In whispered words, our heart condones.

The trees, they listen, boughs so low,
To stories forged in shadows' glow.
With every crack and every sigh,
The soggy ground lets dreams fly high.

A dance of roots, entwining fast,
With memories of a drenched past.
Hidden truths in silence found,
In shadows cast by the soggy ground.

As storm clouds drift and rumbles fade,
In soaking depths, our fears cascade.
Shadowed conversations, soft and round,
In nature's bosom, hope is crowned.

www.ingramcontent.com/pod-product-compliance
Lightning Source LLC
Chambersburg PA
CBHW070723130125
20184CB00031B/1009